M000206239

ONE IDEA PRESS

Ordering Information:
Quantity sales. Special discounts are available on quantity purchases by
corporations, associations, and others. For details, contact the "Special Sales
Department" at the following email address: hello@oneideapress.com.

Paperback Edition: 978-1-944134-47-1
Hardback Edition: 978-1-944134-48-8

Printed in the United States of America

Cancer

a love letter

Heidi Rose Robbins

with illustrations by
Wyoh Lee

hello love.

(yes, you)

Friends,

I'm so glad you are holding this book! It is filled with encouragement and an ongoing invitation for us all to be more fully who we are.

The best way to work with these books is to purchase one for each of your signs — your Sun, Moon, and Rising Sign.

These are the three most important positions in your astrological chart. You can discover what these are if you enter your exact time, date, and place of birth in any online astrology site. Each position has something unique to offer.

When you read the book for your Moon, think of it as an energy that is very available to you. It's a place where you might feel comfortable. The Moon has to do with our emotional life, our patterns of behavior, and circumstances of our childhood. We can rely on the Moon, but we also want to work to shed the patterns that no longer serve us.

The Sun is our present personality. We can learn a lot about our everyday self in the world. We can learn about the energies we have readily available to us to use in service to our highest calling.

The Rising Sign is the most important point. It is the sign that was rising as we took our first breath. It holds the key to our soul's calling. It is an energy we want to cultivate and be generous with throughout our lives.

So — enjoy the journey. Be sure to read them all!

Welcome
{13}

My dear Cancer,

This little book is a love letter to your compassionate, inclusive self. It is written to remind you of your many gifts. It is written to be a loving mirror so any page can remind you who you truly are. Take it in, dear Cancer. It is sometimes vulnerable making to read all the bounty and beauty of you. But promise me you'll take the time to see your sensitive and caring self in these pages.

This little book will also explore those places in ourselves that start to close when we want to open, the part of us that hesitates when we want to act. We all have our quirks and difficulties, after all. But if we return again and again to our potency, vulnerability, and sense of possibility, we can outgrow our closures one by one.

Think of this book as a treasure chest containing the golden coins of YOU. Open it when you wish to remember your beauty, worth or great potential. And remember, too, this Cancerian part of you is just one voice in the symphony of YOU. It cannot possibly contain your complexity and bounty. But it can begin to name just a few of your gifts.

Read this out loud when you can. Read this in the morning. Read it before bed. Read it when you need encouragement. Read it even if you are already feeling at peace. Let it grow your capacity to embody your beauty for all to experience. This little book is yours to read, use and claim! This is your love letter, Cancer. This is the song of YOU.

Big love,
Heidi Rose

Celebrating Cancer

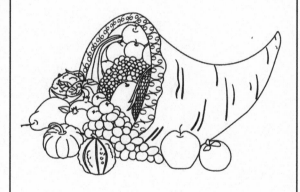

As you read this celebration, you will sometimes say "Yes, yes, yes! This is me!" And you may likewise sometimes feel that you have not fully lived up to some of these qualities! This is honoring and celebrating the very best of your Cancer energy. This is naming the full, conscious, awakened use of your Cancer gifts. We are sounding the note of THE POSSIBLE. So, even if you feel you still have work to do in certain areas — as do we all — let these words be inspiration to offer your best Self!

You feel for all of us.

No other sign is quite as sensitive and emotionally alive as you, dear Cancer. Your tears give others permission to feel. You are FULL with feeling. You deeply understand the pain of another and you embrace others with your empathy.

You are a great nourisher.

Dear Cancer, you make sure those in your midst are taken care of. If they need food, you feed them. If they need love, you listen. If they need clothing, you clothe them. You nourish with compassion and practicality.

You protect your
chosen family.

You are the great defender.
No one dares mess with you or
your brood. Your are fierce in your
ability to safeguard those you
love. Your chosen family often
becomes Humanity itself.

♋

You are inclusive.

No one is left out if you, dear Cancer, are doing the inviting. No one is forgotten. You will pour over your guest list making sure that all have received welcoming. And if anyone needs a place to be, last minute, your door is open. You love inclusively. You include all.

♋

You are Feelingly-Sensitive.

This is one of your super powers.
You feel outward into the world
and receive subtle information
that helps you navigate with
emotional intelligence.
Your feeling powers are
heightened which amplifies your
compassion. You touch and heal
with your sensitivity.

You Feed Others.

Not only do you make a delicious pot of soup out of a cold night, you also feed others with information and care. The kitchen is your hearth and home. But even outside the kitchen, you know just what will help another grow and you provide whatever it takes.

You Build a Lighted House.

You, dear Cancer, are a lighted house for weary souls. You fill your own home and business with light and invite others into your safe haven. You work to shine a light through any darkness, welcoming those who need the light most. You are a shelter.

You are the Great Mama or Papa Bear.

Even if you never choose to have children, you will parent something or someone. Your sign rules birth and parenting. You embody the energy of caretaker, provider, and parent. You are innately responsible and know how to shelter and nourish those you love. You treat Humanity as if it were your child.

You Make Others Feel
At Home.

Home is enormously important to you, so you want others to feel at home when they are with you. You go above and beyond to see that others feel safe and cared for. You create a safe haven and a nourishing retreat.

You love your solo time.

You honor solitude. You know that you need to replenish to offer your truest gifts. You give yourself the time you need to refuel in quiet before taking care of all those who require your care.

You are Resourceful.

You know how to get what you need. You research. You gently inquire. You call up old favors. You know how to find the things that others cannot. You always find a way. You will always lead the way in gathering the needed resources.

♋

You are Tenacious.

You do not give up easily. You see things through. You refuse 'No.' You hold on as long as it takes, dear Cancer. Your tenacity pays off as you continue to offer your love and wisdom.

You love history.

The sign of Cancer rules our past, our history. You have a connection with those that have come before. You like to study and understand what led to this moment. You are particularly connected the lineage of the feminine.

You build your own security.

You are a saver, dear Cancer. You like to tuck money away for a rainy day. You think about contingency plans and always have enough saved for the unexpected. You know how to be frugal to be safe in the long run.

♋

You Are the Great Provider.

What your loved ones need, you will find and provide. It is one of your great joys. You have a great stock of necessities and can offer any and all when called upon. When you choose to invest in something or someone, you offer your financial strength and care.

You are a Great Weaver
of Ideas.

You are not only emotionally
intelligent, you also have the
capacity to hold and combine
many big ideas. You see how many
ideas weave into larger ideas.
You weave together the many
strands of thought into wholeness.

♋

You are Intuitive.

You listen. You receive. You
somehow know. You feel into
what is about to happen. You know
what to say. You touch the
higher realms.

♋

You love a good tradition.

Whether it be Cookie parties,
Thanksgiving recipes or caroling
in the neighborhood, you love
traditional festivities. You love to
honor what was done before you
and what you now carry on.

You make things warm
and cozy.

You are the one waiting at the
door with a mug of hot chocolate
and a warm blanket when your
loved ones return from the cold.
You know how to nest.

You know how to produce an event!

You wrap your arms around an event and take care of everything in your grasp. You think of everything. You care for all those involved. No one should ever underestimate your business acumen. You, dear Cancer, know how to birth an event.

You stand as an Ocean
of Compassion.

You are a vessel of light and
love. You offer your loving-
understanding to all whom you
encounter. You identify with
others and recognize their
pain as your own. When you feel
another suffer, you know you must
act with love.

You stand for wholeness.

You can feel how we are all a part of something greater. You know that any 'part' is a piece of a great whole. You sense the underlying Oneness.

Living Your Cancer Love

How are you feeling, dear Cancer? Can you sense the potency of your gifts? Do you want to make the very most of this compassionate energy of Cancer? Here are some thoughts about how to live fully into your Cancer love and how to nourish your Cancer spirit. Consider them little whispered reminders meant to help you THRIVE. Consider them 'action items' — a loving Cancerian "to-do" list. Consider them invitations to live in the ocean of your sensitivity and care.

Make a pot of soup.

A pot of soup is warm, nourishing and feeds a lot of people. That checks a lot of boxes for you, dear Cancer. You might consider a weekly pot of soup and an invitation to your lighted house where you heal and uplift all who enter.

Light a fire.

Light the fire of your hearth.
You are meant to warm and
nourish. The fire is the heart of
the house and invites your family
and friends to gather. Your own
heart is another kind of hearth.
Invite us in.

♋

Research a distant female
relative or celebrate a
woman in history.

The sign Cancer rules the
feminine lineage. You remind us
of the work of our ancestors. You
call forth the inspiration of the
creators and leaders throughout
history. Tell the stories of the
past. Nourish us with your stories.
Inspire us with the bravery and
kindness of those who have come
before us.

Offer someone shelter.

Shelter can be an actual space to dwell but it can also be the shelter of your love and care. You know how to create a safe place for others to rest and replenish. Open your doors and welcome the weary.

Share your vulnerability.

Your willingness to open will open emotional doors for others. Your willing sensitivity brings relief to those that don't have as easy access to their emotional life. Dare to share what you feel. Your willingness to feel, heals.

♋

Gestate.

You are here to grow things. You are here to birth what you have grown. It could be a baby and it could be a business. Trust the process of gestation. Trust the process of letting it grow.

Growing Your Cancer Love

Sometimes, dear Cancer, we swing too far in one direction and need to invite a balancing energy to set us right. We are all growing and need to address the parts of ourselves that have not developed as fully. The opportunity for Cancer is to invite Capricorn (your opposite sign) into the picture. Here are ways to grow your Cancer love to be more Here are ways to grow your Cancer love to be more decisive, clear and action-oriented.

♋

Reveal Yourself.

At times, dear Cancer, you
have the tendency to hide.
Sometimes you hide in plain site.
Refuse timidity and reveal
your compassionate self. It's a
practice, but a beautiful one.
Practice being willing to be seen.

Don't take it all personally.

This is a tough one because your feelings run so deep. But try to remember that others have a myriad of reasons for saying and doing what they do and say. And often it has nothing to do with you.

Say what you mean.

Simply put, don't stuff your feelings or reactions. Say what you need to say as close to the emotional moment as possible. Otherwise, your behavior will become more reactive or passive aggressive and that doesn't solve anything!

♋

Leave the house.

Of course you love your home, dear Cancer. But it can also be a hiding place. Make sure to boot yourself out your front door now and then to deeply engage. Yes, there is joy in solitude, but learn to leave that safety as well. Confront any fear that stands in your way.

Refuse the feeling of Inferiority

Call in your authority and upright spine and always remember how much you have to offer. You do not need to play small in any way. Play, instead, with your huge compassion and kindness. Come forth as an authority in inclusivity.

Release the wounds
of the past.

It will not serve to stuff and
collect the pain of your past.
I know it's hard to render yourself
vulnerable after heart-ache.
But one of your greatest gifts
is your vulnerability and your
willingness to stay tender. Let go
of any pain that you no longer
need to carry.

Don't let a feeling become a Mood.

It's clear that you feel a lot, dear Cancer. But don't hold fast to any feeling. Let the feeling move through before it becomes a mood. A mood is just a feeling that you stoke or give into. You have to work to keep a mood going. Instead, set it free and welcome in a new feeling.

Cease Worry.

I know it's easy to think that all that worry will amount to something. But it doesn't and it will make you miserable for many hours when you could be engaged in something that brings you joy. When we worry, we are engaged in anticipatory grief. Let's not get ahead of ourselves. Let's stay present in how we can respond proactively in this moment.

Questions to Inspire
Sharing Your Cancer Love

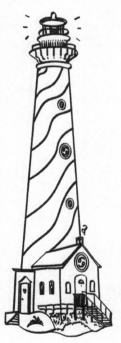

Dear Cancer, here are a few questions and prompts that might inspire or clarify your mission. Grab your journal. Write for 15 minutes about each. Read your answers out loud to a friend. Read them out loud for yourself. Let this exploration foster your Cancerian sensitivity and desire to nourish.

Who and what will I always
care for?
Make a list if you like.

Write about family.

What events, people or groups
are mine to parent,
produce or see over?

I am nourished by...

Where am I being
overly sensitive?

Or Write:
"I feel..."
and explore the full realm
of your current feeling.

What am I protecting?

This is what I need to say...

what would it feel like
to let go?

♋

What am I building
in my life?

If you really knew me,
you'd know,...

One Last Little Love Note:

Cancer, I hope these questions spark new possibility in your life. You have so much to offer, so much to give. And your sensitivity touches so many. If you ever need encouragement, just dip into this little book for a reminder of your light.

Now go forth Cancer, and do your thing.

The World is Waiting for YOU.

Big love,
Heidi Rose

About the Author.

Heidi grew up with an astrologer father and an architect mother. Her father taught her the zodiac with her ABC's and her mother taught her to love art and appreciate the beauty of the natural world. She likes to call herself a poet with a map of the heavens in her pocket. Her passion is to inspire and encourage us all to be our truest, most authentic, radiant selves using the tools of astrology and poetry.

www.heidirose.com
Instagram @heidiroserobbins